Spartanology
Trivia
Challenge

Michigan State Spartans Basketball

**Spartanology Trivia Challenge – Michigan State Spartans Basketball;
First Edition 2008**

Published by
Kick The Ball, Ltd
8595 Columbus Pike, Suite 197
Lewis Center, OH 43035
www.TriviaGameBooks.com

Designed, Formatted, and Edited by: Tom P. Rippey III & Paul F. Wilson
Researched by: Tom P. Rippey III

*For information on ordering this book in bulk at reduced prices, please email us
at pfwilson@trivianthology.com.*

International Standard Book Number: 978-1-934372-40-1

Printed & Bound in the United States of America

Tom P. Rippey III & Paul F. Wilson

Spartanology Trivia Challenge

Michigan State Spartans Basketball

Researched by Tom P. Rippey III

Tom P. Rippey III & Paul F. Wilson, Editors

Kick The Ball, Ltd
Lewis Center, Ohio

This book is dedicated to our families and friends for your unwavering love, support, and your understanding of our pursuit of our passions. Thank you for everything you do for us and for making our lives complete.

Dear Friend,

Thank you for purchasing our *Spartanology Trivia Challenge* game book!

We hope you enjoy it as much as we enjoyed researching and putting it together. This book can be used over and over again in many different ways. One example would be to use it in a head-to-head challenge by alternating questions between Spartan basketball fans – or by playing as teams. Another option would be to simply challenge yourself to see how many questions you could answer correctly. No matter how you choose to use this book, you'll have fun and maybe even learn a fact or two about Spartans basketball.

We have made every attempt to verify the accuracy of the questions and answers contained in this book. However it is still possible that from time to time an error has been made by us or our researchers. In the event you find a question or answer that is questionable or inaccurate, we ask for your understanding and thank you for bringing it to our attention so that we may improve future editions of this book. Please email us at tprippey@trivianthology.com with those observations and comments.

Have fun playing *Spartanology Trivia Challenge*!

Tom & Paul

Tom Rippey & Paul Wilson
Co-Founders, Kick The Ball, Ltd

PS – You can discover more about all of our current trivia game books by visiting us online at www.TriviaGameBooks.com.

Table of Contents

SPARTANOLOGY TRIVIA CHALLENGE

How to Play

Book Format:

There are four quarters, each made up of fifty questions. Each quarter's questions have assigned point values. Questions are designed to get progressively more difficult as you proceed through each quarter, as well as through the book itself. Most questions are in a four-option multiple-choice format so that you will at least have a 25% chance of getting a correct answer for some of the more challenging questions.

We've even added an *Overtime* section in the event of a tie, or just in case you want to keep playing a little longer.

Game Options:

One Player -
To play on your own, simply answer each of the questions in all the quarters, and in the overtime section, if you'd like. Use the *Player / Team Score Sheet* to record your answers and the quarter *Answer Keys* to check your answers. Calculate each quarter's points and the total for the game at the bottom of the *Player / Team Score Sheet* to determine your final score.

Two or More Players –
To play with multiple players decide if you will all be competing with each other individually, or if you will form and play as teams. Each player / team will then have its own *Player / Team Score Sheet* to record its answer. You can use the quarter *Answer Keys* to check your answers and to calculate your final scores.

The *Player / Team Score Sheets* have been designed so that each team can answer all questions or you can divide the questions up in any combination you would prefer. For example, you may want to alternate questions if two players are playing or answer every third question for three players, etc. In any case, simply record your response to your questions in the corresponding quarter and question number on the *Player / Team Score Sheet*.

A winner will be determined by multiplying the total number of correct answers for each quarter by the point value per quarter, then adding together the final total for all quarters combined. Play the game again and again by alternating the questions that your team is assigned so that you will answer a different set of questions each time you play.

You Create the Game -
There are countless other ways of using **Spartanology Trivia Challenge** questions. It's limited only to your imagination. Examples might be using them at your tailgate or other college basketball related party. Players / Teams who answer questions incorrectly may have to perform a required action, or winners may receive special prizes. Let us know what other games you come up with!

Have fun!

1) What year did the nickname Spartans become widely associated with Michigan State?

    A) 1894
    B) 1907
    C) 1919
    D) 1926

2) What are the Spartans' official colors?

    A) Green and Ivory
    B) Forest Green and White
    C) Green and White
    D) Hunter Green and Ivory

3) What is the name of MSU's arena?

    A) Crisler Arena
    B) Breslin Center
    C) Rose Arena
    D) Convocation Center

4) How many Naismith College Player of the Year winners played at Michigan State?

    A) 0
    B) 2
    C) 4
    D) 5

5) What is the name of the Michigan State fight song?

    A) "Fight On Spartans"
    B) "Victory Today"
    C) "Fight, State, Fight"
    D) "MSU Fight Song"

6) How many MSU players have won an Olympic gold medal for basketball?

    A) 2
    B) 4
    C) 6
    D) 9

7) How many times has Michigan State appeared in the NCAA Final Four?

    A) 3
    B) 6
    C) 9
    D) 12

8) Who had the longest coaching tenure at Michigan State?

    A) Jud Heathcote
    B) Gus Ganakas
    C) Benjamin VanAlstyne
    D) Forrest Anderson

Preseason

9) Which season did Michigan State first play in the Big Ten conference?

    A)   1928-29
    B)   1943-44
    C)   1950-51
    D)   1957-58

10) What year did the Spartans play their first game?

    A)   1899
    B)   1903
    C)   1911
    D)   1917

11) Who led the Spartans in total rebounds in the 2007-08 season?

    A)   Drew Naymick
    B)   Raymar Morgan
    C)   Marquise Gray
    D)   Goran Suton

12) The seating capacity of the Breslin Center is greater than 15,000.

    A)   True
    B)   False

13) What is the name of Michigan State's costumed mascot?

A) Sparty
B) Caesar
C) Spartacus
D) Adonis

14) Who is the play-by-play radio man for the Spartan Sports Network?

A) Gus Ganakas
B) Dave Revsine
C) Will Tieman
D) Mark Silverman

15) Which season did MSU play its first overtime game?

A) 1909-10
B) 1925-26
C) 1931-32
D) 1946-47

16) Which Big Ten opponent has Michigan State played the most?

A) Ohio State
B) Michigan
C) Minnesota
D) Illinois

17) Did Michigan State score greater than 2,500 points as a team in the 2007-08 season?

    A) Yes
    B) No

18) Who was MSU's opponent in the 2000 NCAA Tournament Championship Game?

    A) Georgetown
    B) UCLA
    C) North Carolina
    D) Florida

19) What was Michigan State originally known as?

    A) Michigan Agricultural College
    B) Michigan College of Science
    C) State University of Michigan
    D) Michigan State Agricultural College

20) Who was the first consensus First Team All-American at Michigan State?

    A) Johnny Green
    B) Terry Furlow
    C) Magic Johnson
    D) Greg Kelser

21) Did Michigan State have a winning record their first season?

    A) Yes
    B) No

22) When did Earvin Johnson get nicknamed "Magic"?

    A) As a toddler
    B) After a middle school talent show
    C) Following a high school basketball game
    D) After his debut with Michigan State

23) Which Michigan State coach has the most all-time career wins?

    A) Tom Izzo
    B) Forrest Anderson
    C) John Benington
    D) Jud Heathcote

24) Which of the following Spartans was not chosen to the NCAA All-Tournament Team in 2000?

    A) Morris Peterson
    B) Jason Richardson
    C) Charlie Bell
    D) A.J. Granger

25) Who holds the MSU record for assists in a single game?

    A)   Eric Snow
    B)   Magic Johnson
    C)   Gary Ganakas
    D)   Mateen Cleaves

26) When was MSU's first undefeated season (min. 5 games)?

    A)   1902-03
    B)   1909-10
    C)   1921-22
    D)   1925-26

27) What is the MSU record for most consecutive NCAA Tournament appearances?

    A)   7
    B)   9
    C)   11
    D)   13

28) Magic Johnson led the Spartans in scoring for the 1978-79 championship season.

    A)   True
    B)   False

Preseason *1-Point Questions*

29) How many seasons did Michigan State play without a head coach?

    A) 1
    B) 3
    C) 5
    D) 8

30) Which opponent did MSU face in the first round of the 2008 Big Ten Tournament?

    A) Minnesota
    B) Wisconsin
    C) Iowa
    D) Ohio State

31) Where did MSU play before the Breslin Center?

    A) University Arena
    B) Convocation Center
    C) Jenison Fieldhouse
    D) Rose Arena

32) In how many overtime games did MSU play in 2007-08?

    A) 0
    B) 1
    C) 3
    D) 4

33) Did Michigan State go undefeated at home in the 2007-08 season?

    A) Yes
    B) No

34) What is the name of the Spartan Statue that can be found on the MSU campus?

    A) Spartacus
    B) Leonidas
    C) Archidamos
    D) Spartan

35) Which opponent scored the most points against Michigan State in the 2007-08 season?

    A) Penn State
    B) Indiana
    C) Memphis
    D) Illinois

36) How many seasons has Michigan State led the nation in total team rebounds?

    A) 2
    B) 4
    C) 5
    D) 8

37) Which opposing player holds the record for most points scored in a single game against Michigan State?

    A) Isiah Thomas
    B) John Havlicek
    C) Larry Bird
    D) Jimmy Rayl

38) Michigan State has won more Big Ten Tournament Titles than any other Big Ten school.

    A) True
    B) False

39) What is the nickname of the student section at the Breslin Center?

    A) Hearty Sparty's
    B) Greenies
    C) Fear Zone
    D) Izzone

40) When was the only season the Spartans did not play basketball since 1899?

    A) 1917-18
    B) 1939-40
    C) 1943-44
    D) 1968-69

41) How many NCAA National Championships has Michigan State won?

    A) 1
    B) 2
    C) 4
    D) 6

42) Who is the only Spartan player to be named Academic All-American of the Year?

    A) Chris Hill
    B) Ralph Simpson
    C) Jason Andreas
    D) Greg Kelser

43) Who was the Spartans' first opponent at the Breslin Center?

    A) Detroit
    B) Evansville
    C) Nebraska
    D) Eastern Michigan

44) What is the total number of seasons the Spartans have gone undefeated at the Breslin Center?

    A) 2
    B) 4
    C) 6
    D) 8

45) Who holds the MSU record for career blocked shots?

    A) Matt Steigenga
    B) Andre Hutson
    C) Aloysius Anagonye
    D) Drew Naymick

46) Which season did Michigan State have two Consensus All-Americans?

    A) 1978-79
    B) 1986-87
    C) 1999-00
    D) 2002-03

47) What is the MSU record for most losses in a single season at the Breslin Center?

    A) 3
    B) 5
    C) 7
    D) 9

48) Who holds the Michigan State record for points scored in a single game?

    A) Shawn Respert
    B) Maurice Ager
    C) Scott Skiles
    D) Terry Furlow

49) Do the Spartans have an all-time winning record in overtime games?

    A) Yes
    B) No

50) What year did Michigan State first celebrate a victory over Michigan?

    A) 1909
    B) 1915
    C) 1920
    D) 1928

Preseason Spartan Cool Fact

The first five Michigan State basketball head coaches held many responsibilities within the university. MSU's first head coach, Charles Bemies, was also athletic director and head coach of the football, baseball, and track teams. The second head coach, George Denman, was also head football coach. The third head coach, Chester Brewster, was athletic director and head coach of the baseball and football teams. The fourth head coach, John Macklin, also coached the football team. MSU's fifth head coach, George Gauthier, was assistant athletic director and head football coach. These first five Spartan head coaches combined for an overall record of 175-103 in basketball for a .629 winning percentage. As head football coaches, these five combined for an overall record of 101-47-2 for a .680 winning percentage. Even though the game is much more complex today, this is still a great accomplishment for these five head coaches.

Preseason Answer Key

1) D – 1926 (A contest was held to select a new nickname and the name chosen was Michigan Staters. The sports editor of the Lansing State Journal felt this to be too burdensome and picked Spartans from one of the entries.)

2) C – Green and White (These colors became widely associated with MSU in 1903.)

3) B – Breslin Center (It opened in 1984 at a cost of $43 million.)

4) A – 0 (The Naismith Trophy was first awarded in 1969 and no MSU players have won the award.)

5) D – "MSU Fight Song" (The song was written by Francis Irving Lankey in 1915.)

6) A – 2 (Magic Johnson won a gold with the Dream Team in 1992 and Steve Smith won gold in 2000.)

7) B – 6 (1957, 1979, 1999-01, and 2005)

8) C – Benjamin VanAlstyne (He coached the Spartans for 22 seasons from the 1926-27 to the 1948-49 seasons.)

9) C – 1950-51 (MSU finished 5-9 and 7th overall in their first season of Big Ten conference play.)

10) A – 1899 (The Spartans lost 6-7 to the Olivet Comets on Feb. 27, 1899.)

11) D – Goran Suton (He led the team with 295 total rebounds [101 offensive and 194 defensive].)

12) B – False (The Breslin Center has an official seating capacity of 14,759.)

13) A – Sparty (He first appeared at a football game in 1989 and is now one of the most recognized symbols of the university.)

14) C – Will Tieman (He has served ten seasons as the Spartans play-by-play radio man [1992-93 to 1995-96 and from 2002-03 to 2007-08].)

15) D – 1946-47 (MSU beat Syracuse 61-57 on Dec. 31, 1946.)

16) B – Michigan (The Spartans have played the Wolverines 162 times.)

17) A – Yes (The Spartans scored a total of 2,564 points for an average of 71.2 points per game.)

18) D – Florida (The top-seeded Spartans beat the fifth-seeded Gators 89-76.)

19) A – Michigan Agricultural College (The first land grant college, MSU was founded in 1855 and went by the name Michigan Agricultural College until 1925.)

20) C – Magic Johnson (He was a Consensus First Team All-American in 1979. Two other Spartans have been named Consensus First Team All-Americans: Shawn Respert [1995] and Mateen Cleaves [2000].)

21) B – No (The Spartans played two games against Olivet and lost both meetings [6-7 and 6-15].)

22) C – Following a high school basketball game (Earvin recorded a triple double as a sophomore and a sports writer for the Lansing State Journal dubbed him "Magic".)

23) D – Jud Heathcote (He led the Spartans to 340 wins from 1976-95.)

24) B – Jason Richardson (Morris Peterson, A.J. Granger, Charlie Bell, Mateen Cleaves, and Udonis Haslem of Florida made up the All-Tournament Team in 2000.)

25) D – Mateen Cleaves (He had 20 assists against Michigan in 2000.)

26) A – 1902-03 (MSU finished the season 6-0.)

27) C – 11 (The Spartans appeared in the NCAA Tournament every year from 1998-2008.)

28) B – False (Greg Kelser led the team with 602 points for an average of 18.8 points per game. Johnson had 548 points for an average of 17.1 points per game.)

29) A – 1 (The only season MSU played without a head coach was the first season [1899].)

30) D – Ohio State (The Spartans beat the Buckeyes 67-60 before losing to Wisconsin 63-65 in the second round.)

31) C – Jenison Fieldhouse (This sporting venue opened in 1940. Capacity for Spartan basketball games was 10,004.)

32) A – 0 (MSU has gone two straight seasons without playing an overtime game.)

33) A – Yes (MSU went a perfect 17-0 at home.)

34) D – Spartan (The statue stands 10'6" tall and weighs three tons. Nicknamed "Sparty", the statue can be found about a half mile north east of the Breslin Center.)

35) C – Memphis (The Spartans lost 74-92 to the Tigers in the third round of the NCAA Tournament.)

36) A – 2 (The Spartans led the nation in 1999-00 with 39.0 rebounds per game and again in 2000-01 with 42.5 rebounds per game.)

37) D – Jimmy Rayl (He scored 56 points for Indiana in 1963 [MSU 94, IU 113].)

38) B – False (MSU has won two tournament titles [1999 & 2000]. Ohio State, Wisconsin, Iowa, and Illinois also have two titles apiece.)

39) D – Izzone (With over 3,000 members, this rowdy student section helps give the Spartans a home court advantage.)

40) C – 1943-44 (The season was suspended due to World War II.)

41) B – 2 (1979 and 2000)

42) A – Chris Hill (He won this honor in 2005. Chris was also First Team Academic All-American in 2004 and Third Team in 2003.)

43) C – Nebraska (MSU beat the Cornhuskers 80-69 in the first game at the Breslin Center.)

44) B – 4 (MSU went undefeated at the Breslin Center in 1998-99, 1999-00, 2000-01, & 2007-08.)

45) D – Drew Naymick (He recorded 134 blocked shots from the 2004-05 season through the 2007-08 season.)

46) C – 1999-00 (Mateen Cleaves and Morris Peterson were both Consensus Second Team All-Americans.)

47) B – 5 (The Spartans went 9-5 at home in the 1992-93 season and 10-5 in the 1995-96 season.)

48) D – Terry Furlow (He scored 50 points against Iowa in 1976 [MSU 105, Iowa 88].)

49) B – No (MSU is 38-39 all-time in overtime games for a .494 winning percentage.)

50) A – 1909 (The Spartans beat the Wolverines 24-16 in their first-ever meeting.)

Note: All answers valid as of the end of the 2007-08 season, unless otherwise indicated in the question itself.

Regular Season

2-Point Questions

1) How many times has MSU scored 100 or more points in a single game?

   A) 25
   B) 32
   C) 39
   D) 47

2) Which Michigan State player led the team in assists in the 2007-08 season?

   A) Kalin Lucas
   B) Drew Neitzel
   C) Travis Walton
   D) Chris Allen

3) Which head coach had the second longest tenure at Michigan State?

   A) Tom Izzo
   B) Forrest Anderson
   C) John Benington
   D) Jud Heathcote

4) How many different decades has Michigan State won at least 175 games?

   A) 1
   B) 2
   C) 4
   D) 6

Regular Season *2-Point Questions*

5) What was the name of the first athletic conference to which Michigan State belonged?

    A) Michigan Intercollegiate Athletic Conference
    B) Eastern College Athletic Conference
    C) Great Lakes Valley Conference
    D) Heartland Conference

6) Has Michigan State ever played 40 or more games in a single season?

    A) Yes
    B) No

7) Which opposing player holds the record for most rebounds against Michigan State in a single game?

    A) Don Kojis
    B) Wilt Chamberlin
    C) Clark Kellogg
    D) Juwan Howard

8) What is MSU's record for largest margin of victory over an opponent?

    A) 69 points
    B) 75 points
    C) 81 points
    D) 99 points

9) Which team did MSU play in the 1979 NCAA Tournament Championship game?

    A) Penn
    B) Texas A&M
    C) Mississippi State
    D) Indiana State

10) Has Michigan State ever lost to any of the U.S. Service Academies?

    A) Yes
    B) No

11) What is Michigan State's winning percentage against Michigan?

    A) .367
    B) .438
    C) .506
    D) .561

12) Which non-conference opponent has Michigan State played the most?

    A) Case Western
    B) Detroit
    C) Missouri
    D) Notre Dame

Regular Season *2-Point Questions*

13) Has Michigan State ever won a game that went into triple overtime?

   A) Yes
   B) No

14) Who holds the Michigan State career record for points scored?

   A) Magic Johnson
   B) Terry Furlow
   C) Shawn Respert
   D) Morris Peterson

15) Who was the last Spartan player to record a triple double?

   A) Drew Neitzel
   B) Shawn Respert
   C) Charlie Bell
   D) Magic Johnson

16) Which team handed Michigan State its worst loss ever?

   A) Wake Forest
   B) Olivet
   C) Xavier
   D) Indiana

Regular Season *2-Point Questions*

17) How many times has Michigan State beaten a team ranked #1 in the *AP* Poll?

    A) 0
    B) 2
    C) 4
    D) 7

18) In the 2007-08 season, what were the fewest points Michigan State allowed in a single game?

    A) 41
    B) 44
    C) 47
    D) 52

19) What is MSU's longest winning streak in the Michigan State-Michigan series?

    A) 6 games
    B) 8 games
    C) 11 games
    D) 13 games

20) Have the Spartans won 50 or more NCAA Tournament games?

    A) Yes
    B) No

21) Who was the last player to be a three-time team MVP for the Spartans?

- A) Sam Vincent
- B) William Kilgore
- C) Mateen Cleaves
- D) Steve Smith

22) How many *AP* Top-10 finishes does MSU have?

- A) 7
- B) 9
- C) 11
- D) 14

23) Michigan State has never lost a game when scoring 100 or more points.

- A) True
- B) False

24) What are the all-time fewest points a Michigan State team has allowed in a single game?

- A) 0
- B) 2
- C) 3
- D) 7

25) Which MSU head coach has the second most all-time career wins?

    A) Chester Brewer
    B) Forrest Anderson
    C) Benjamin VanAlstyne
    D) Tom Izzo

26) Did the Spartans have a game in the 2007-08 season in which they scored fewer than 50 points?

    A) Yes
    B) No

27) When was the last season the Spartans shot .500 or more from the field?

    A) 1978-79
    B) 1999-00
    C) 2003-04
    D) 2007-08

28) What is MSU's record for consecutive non-losing seasons?

    A) 16
    B) 20
    C) 24
    D) 32

29) How many of Michigan State's all-time NCAA Tournament games have gone into overtime?

A) 2
B) 4
C) 6
D) 7

30) Since 1980, has any Spartan player recorded 25 or more rebounds in a single game?

A) Yes
B) No

31) Who was Michigan State's first NCAA Tournament opponent?

A) Kansas
B) Providence
C) San Francisco
D) Notre Dame

32) How many times have Michigan State players been named Big Ten Player of the Year?

A) 3
B) 5
C) 6
D) 9

33) What is Michigan State's team record for most three-pointers made in a single game?

    A) 12
    B) 16
    C) 18
    D) 21

34) How many times has Michigan State played in the Postseason NIT Tournament?

    A) 2
    B) 4
    C) 5
    D) 7

35) How many points was MSU's largest loss to Michigan?

    A) 28
    B) 36
    C) 41
    D) 57

36) How many times has Michigan State finished #1 in the last *AP* Poll?

    A) 0
    B) 2
    C) 3
    D) 4

37) Who led the Spartans in free-throw percentage in the 2007-08 season (minimum 50 attempts)?

    A) Travis Walton
    B) Durrell Summers
    C) Goran Suton
    D) Drew Neitzel

38) Who was the only Spartan to be named Big Ten Player of the Week more than once for the 2007-08 season?

    A) Raymar Morgan
    B) Goran Suton
    C) Drew Neitzel
    D) Marquise Gray

39) Magic Johnson is the only Spartan to have recorded 70 or more steals in a single season.

    A) True
    B) False

40) Which season did the Spartans first record 20 wins?

    A) 1919-20
    B) 1937-38
    C) 1956-57
    D) 1963-64

Regular Season 2-Point Questions

41) Against which conference opponent does Michigan State have the most wins?

- A) Penn State
- B) Wisconsin
- C) Michigan
- D) Northwestern

42) Which team did the Spartans play in the first round of the 2008 NCAA Tournament?

- A) Pitt
- B) Memphis
- C) Temple
- D) Marquette

43) Who holds MSU's career record for most games played?

- A) Chris Bell
- B) Mateen Cleaves
- C) Andre Hutson
- D) Antonio Smith

44) What is MSU's record for most consecutive Big Ten regular-season titles?

- A) 2
- B) 4
- C) 5
- D) 7

45) Has a Michigan State player ever led the nation in scoring?

    A) Yes
    B) No

46) What is Michigan State's all-time consecutive home wins record?

    A) 44
    B) 47
    C) 53
    D) 61

47) In the 2007-08 season, how many Spartans averaged 10 or more points per game?

    A) 1
    B) 3
    C) 4
    D) 6

48) Which non-conference opponent has the most wins against Michigan State?

    A) North Carolina
    B) Kentucky
    C) Butler
    D) Notre Dame

49) What season did Michigan State win its first regular
season Big Ten title?

    A) 1956-57
    B) 1961-62
    C) 1965-66
    D) 1970-71

50) Has Michigan State ever played in the Jimmy V Classic?

    A) Yes
    B) No

Regular Season Spartan Cool Fact

Tom Izzo is well known for his success at Michigan State as well as his commitment to academics, graduating 86% of his players that complete eligibility. However, Izzo's commitment to others goes well beyond the Spartan family. In 2005, Izzo joined Jay Bilas and seven other head coaches in an organized tournament called "Operation Hardwood". This tournament took place in Kuwait with the teams consisting of U.S troops. The coaches also held basketball clinics for Kuwaiti children. Izzo coached the Camp Arifjan team and did not lose a game during the entire tournament, winning 54-39 in the finals. Upon his return, he is quoted as saying, "It might sound hokey, but I know I'll be a better person and American for going over there." Izzo also participated in the second Operation Hardwood in 2006.

Regular Season Answer Key

1) C – 39 (The last time the Spartans passed the century mark was in 2007-08 when they beat Indiana 103-74.)

2) C – Travis Walton (He led the team with 156 assists.)

3) D – Jud Heathcote (He coached the Spartans from the 1976-77 season through the 1994-95 season.)

4) B – 2 (MSU won 214 games in the 1990s and 217 games so far this decade.)

5) A – Michigan Intercollegiate Athletic Conference (Founded in 1888, this is the oldest athletic conference in the nation. MSU was a founding member along with Olivet, Albion, and Hillsdale. The Spartans left the conference in 1907.)

6) B – No (The most games MSU played in a single season was 39 in 1999-00. The Spartans finished 32-7.)

7) A – Don Kojis (He recorded 23 rebounds for Marquette in 1959 [MSU 74, Marquette 69].)

8) D – 99 points (MSU beat Alma College 102-3 in 1902.)

9) D – Indiana State (The second-seeded Spartans beat the top-seeded Sycamores 75-64.)

10) A – Yes (MSU lost 90-91 [OT] to Navy in 1986. The Spartans are 1-0 against Army, 0-1 against Navy, and have never played Air Force.)

11) B – .438 (Michigan State has an all-time record of 71-91 against the Wolverines.)

12) D – Notre Dame (The Spartans have played the Fighting Irish in a total of 94 games. The last time the two teams met was in the third round of the 1979 NCAA Tournament.)

13) A – Yes (The Spartans are 1-5 in triple-overtime games. The only win was against Ohio State in 1988 [MSU 78, OSU 77].)

14) C – Shawn Respert (He scored a total of 2,531 points from 1990-95.)

15) C – Charlie Bell (He recorded one career triple double against Oakland on Nov. 19, 2000. The only other Spartan to have a triple double is Magic Johnson [8 times].)

16) D – Indiana (The Spartans fell 55-107 to the Hoosiers on Jan. 4, 1975.)

17) B – 2 (The third-ranked Spartans beat Indiana St. 75-64 in the 1979 NCAA Championship game. An unranked MSU team beat top-ranked Wisconsin 64-55 on Feb. 20, 2007.)

18) A – 41 (The Spartans held Illinois to 41 points on Jan. 30th [MSU 51, Illinois 41].)

19) B – 8 games (The Spartans beat the Wolverines every meeting from Feb. 2, 1998 to Jan. 30, 2002.)

20) B – No (Michigan State has an all-time record of 43-21 in the NCAA Tournament for a .672 winning percentage.)

21) C – Mateen Cleaves (He was team MVP from 1998-2000. The other three listed along with Albert Ferrari, are the only other players to be team MVP three times.)

22) A – 7 (1957 [7th], 1978 [4th], 1979 [3rd], 1990 [4th], 1999 [2nd], 2000 [2nd], & 2001 [3rd])

23) B – False (The Spartans lost 106-109 to Gonzaga in triple overtime on Nov. 22, 2005.)

24) A – 0 (MSU beat the Governor's Guard 19-0 on Feb. 15, 1902.)

25) D – Tom Izzo (He has led the Spartans to 305 wins since the 1995-96 season.)

26) A – Yes (The Spartans managed only 36 points against Iowa on Jan. 12th and 42 points against Wisconsin on Feb. 28th.)

27) C – 2003-04 (Michigan State made 689 of 1,510 shots from the field for a percentage made of .546.)

28) B – 20 (The last time Spartans had a losing season was when they finished 10-18 in the 1987-88 season.)

29) C – 6 (MSU is 2-4 in NCAA Tournament overtime games. The Spartans wins came against Murray State in the first round of the 1990 Tournament and vs. Kentucky in 2-OT in the 2005 Regional Final.)

30) B – No (Spartan players have recorded 25 or more rebounds in a single game nine times. Greg Kelser was the last player to do so with 27 rebounds against Wisconsin on Jan. 3, 1976.)

31) D – Notre Dame (MSU beat the Fighting Irish 85-83 in the first round of the 1957 NCAA Tournament.)

32) C – 6 (Jay Vincent [1981], Scott Skiles [1986], Shawn Respert [1995], Mateen Cleaves [1998 and 1999], & Morris Peterson [2000])

33) B – 16 (MSU shot 16 of 32 from 3-point range against Michigan on March 4, 2000.)

34) C – 5 (MSU appeared in the NIT Tournament in 1983, 1989, 1993, 1996, & 1997.)

35) C – 41 (The Spartans lost 28-69 to the Wolverines on March 6, 1948.)

36) A – 0 (The highest MSU has finished in the final *AP* Poll is second in 1999 and 2000. The *AP* does not have a post-NCAA Tournament poll.)

37) D – Drew Neitzel (He went 74-86 from the line for a .860 percentage made.)

38) A – Raymar Morgan (He was named player of the week for Nov. 19th and Jan. 7th. The only other Spartans named Big Ten Player of the Week were Neitzel [Jan. 28th] and Suton [March 3rd].)

39) B – False (Magic recorded 71 steals in the 1977-78 season and 75 steals in the 1978-79 season. Mateen Cleaves is the only other Spartan to reach 70 steals in a season after recording 73 in the 1997-98 season.)

40) A – 1919-20 (MSU finished the season 21-15 for a .583 winning percentage.)

41) D – Northwestern (MSU has an overall record of 76-36 against the Wildcats for a .679 winning percentage.)

42) C – Temple (The Spartans beat the Owls 72-61 before losing to Memphis 74-92 in the third round.)

43) A – Chris Bell (He played in 140 games with MSU from 1997-2001.)

44) B – 4 (Michigan State won the Big Ten regular-season title from 1997-98 through 2000-01.)

45) B – No (The closest was Scott Skiles in the 1985-86 season when he finished second in the nation with 850 total points scored.)

46) C – 53 (MSU won 53 home games spanning the 1998-99 to 2001-02 seasons.)

47) B – 3 (Raymar Morgan [14.0], Drew Neitzel [13.9], & Kalin Lucas [10.3])

48) D – Notre Dame (MSU has an all-time record of 35-59 against the Fighting Irish for a .362 winning percentage.)

49) A – 1956-57 (After starting conference play 0-3, the Spartans won ten of their last eleven to finish 10-4, capturing their first Big Ten title.)

50) A – Yes (The Spartans beat Seton Hall 72-57 in 2000 and Boston College 77-70 in 2005.)

Note: All answers valid as of the end of the 2007-08 season, unless otherwise indicated in the question itself.

Conference Tournament *3-Point Questions*

1) How many times has Michigan State appeared in the Big Ten Tournament Championship game?

    A) 1
    B) 2
    C) 4
    D) 6

2) Who holds MSU's record for free throws made in a single game?

    A) Terry Furlow
    B) Sam Vincent
    C) Goran Suton
    D) Al Ferrari

3) Which season did the Spartans first record 30 wins?

    A) 1978-79
    B) 1990-91
    C) 1998-99
    D) 2004-05

4) Did any Spartan have greater than 50 steals in the entire 2007-08 season?

    A) Yes
    B) No

Conference Tournament *3-Point Questions*

5) From which country was the only international team the Spartans have played?

    A) Japan
    B) Cuba
    C) Mexico
    D) Russia

6) What is the MSU record for most consecutive winning seasons?

    A) 8
    B) 10
    C) 12
    D) 14

7) Did MSU hold Larry Bird to less than .500 from the field in the 1979 NCAA Tournament Championship game?

    A) Yes
    B) No

8) In the MSU Fight Song, where is the school known to all?

    A) In those that live green and white
    B) In the center of courage
    C) In the land of beauty
    D) On the banks of the Red Cedar

Conference Tournament *3-Point Questions*

9) What is MSU's record for consecutive home-opening wins?

    A) 16
    B) 21
    C) 25
    D) 31

10) In which decade were the most Spartans named Consensus First or Second Team All-American?

    A) 1950s
    B) 1970s
    C) 1990s
    D) 2000s

11) Who holds the Michigan State record for steals in a career?

    A) Mark Montgomery
    B) Mateen Cleaves
    C) Ken Redfield
    D) Eric Snow

12) Who is the only Spartan to score 20 or more points in their freshman debut?

    A) Magic Johnson
    B) Raymar Morgan
    C) Jay Vincent
    D) Charlie Bell

13) Who coached the Spartans immediately prior to Jud Heathcote?

A) John Benington
B) Forrest Anderson
C) Gus Ganakas
D) Peter Newell

14) Has Michigan State ever had a player drafted number one overall in the NBA Draft?

A) Yes
B) No

15) What is the only team MSU played more than once and never beaten in the NCAA Tournament?

A) Duke
B) Kentucky
C) UCLA
D) North Carolina

16) Who was MSU's only international player on the 2007-08 roster?

A) Isaiah Dahlman
B) Tom Herzog
C) Idong Ibok
D) Goran Suton

17) Did Jud Heathcote coach the Spartans to more than 20 wins in his last season?

    A) Yes
    B) No

18) Which team snapped MSU's record for consecutive home wins?

    A) Oklahoma
    B) Cornell
    C) Eastern Washington
    D) Wisconsin

19) In the MSU Alma Mater, what do we watch grow?

    A) Fields of wheat
    B) Team pride
    C) Points
    D) Success

20) Who was Michigan State's first official basketball coach?

    A) Fred Walker
    B) Charles Bemies
    C) Peter Newell
    D) John Kobs

21) Against which team was the last regular-season Big Ten loss for the Spartans in 2007-08 season?

    A) Illinois
    B) Michigan
    C) Purdue
    D) Ohio State

22) Was Magic Johnson ever a team captain at Michigan State?

    A) Yes
    B) No

23) How many total years has MSU made the NCAA Tournament?

    A) 22
    B) 26
    C) 30
    D) 35

24) Since 1938, what is the MSU record for fewest points scored in a game?

    A) 11
    B) 14
    C) 18
    D) 23

25) How many times have Michigan State coaches been named *AP* Coach of the Year?

    A) 1
    B) 2
    C) 4
    D) 5

26) How many times has Michigan State appeared in the NCAA Tournament Championship game?

    A) 2
    B) 3
    C) 5
    D) 6

27) What is the MSU record for most consecutive regular season Big Ten Championships?

    A) 3
    B) 4
    C) 6
    D) 8

28) Who was the first African-American player to sign with Michigan State?

    A) Julius McCoy
    B) Stan Washington
    C) Bill Kilgore
    D) Rickey Ayala

29) What is the MSU record for most consecutive Big Ten losses?

    A) 7
    B) 9
    C) 11
    D) 14

30) Has Michigan State ever gone undefeated in the Big Ten?

    A) Yes
    B) No

31) Who scored the most points for MSU in the 2008 NCAA Tournament?

    A) Chris Allen
    B) Goran Sutton
    C) Drew Neitzel
    D) Raymar Morgan

32) What is the MSU record for most points scored in a non-overtime game?

    A) 121
    B) 128
    C) 136
    D) 140

33) When was the last time a #1-ranked Michigan State team lost to an unranked opponent?

    A) 1978-79
    B) 1990-91
    C) 1997-98
    D) 2000-01

34) Who was the last Spartan to earn the honor of Big Ten Scoring Champion?

    A) Drew Neitzel
    B) Jason Richardson
    C) Paul Davis
    D) Marcus Taylor

35) After whom is the Michigan State Inspirational Player Award named?

    A) Stephen G. Scofes
    B) Dr. James Feurig
    C) Antonio Smith
    D) Tim Bograkos

36) Who is the only Spartan head coach to last one season or less?

    A) Peter Newell
    B) Fred Walker
    C) Alton Kircher
    D) Gus Ganakas

Conference Tournament *3-Point Questions*

37) Which player holds the MSU record for blocks in a single season?

- A) Drew Naymick
- B) Paul Davis
- C) Ken Johnson
- D) George Papadakos

38) Which team gave MSU its first home loss at the Breslin Center?

- A) Bowling Green
- B) Nebraska
- C) Austin Peay
- D) Detroit

39) Which Big Ten school has the best winning percentage against the Spartans?

- A) Northwestern
- B) Purdue
- C) Ohio State
- D) Indiana

40) Did Michigan State win the last game played at Jenison Fieldhouse?

- A) Yes
- B) No

Conference Tournament *3-Point Questions*

41) What is the MSU record for most consecutive NCAA Tournament wins?

    A) 6
    B) 8
    C) 10
    D) 13

42) Who is the only Spartan to have won the Frances Pomeroy Naismith Award?

    A) Mateen Cleaves
    B) Mike Robinson
    C) Benny White
    D) John Bailey

43) Who holds the MSU record for best career free-throw percentage?

    A) Magic Johnson
    B) Scott Skiles
    C) Drew Neitzel
    D) Larry Polec

44) Jud Heathcote has a jersey number retired in his honor.

    A) True
    B) False

45) Who was the first Spartan to appear on the cover of *Sports Illustrated*?

    A) Mateen Cleaves
    B) Greg Kelser
    C) Magic Johnson
    D) Shawn Respert

46) What is inscribed on the base of the Spartan statue?

    A) Sports figures
    B) Lyrics to the MSU Fight Song
    C) Welcome to MSU
    D) Name of the artist

47) How many career NCAA Tournament rebounds did Johnny Green record from 1957-59?

    A) 82
    B) 99
    C) 107
    D) 118

48) How many Spartans are in the Naismith Memorial Basketball Hall of Fame as players?

    A) 1
    B) 2
    C) 4
    D) 5

Conference Tournament *3-Point Questions*

49) In the 2007-08 season, how many times did the Spartans win a game when trailing at halftime?

  A) 1
  B) 3
  C) 5
  D) 8

50) What is the Michigan State record for most consecutive Big Ten wins?

  A) 12
  B) 15
  C) 18
  D) 22

Conference Tournament Spartan Cool Fact

On Dec. 13, 2003, Michigan State and Kentucky faced off in the first ever "BasketBowl". The game took place at Ford Field in Detroit and set an all-time attendance record for basketball with 78,129. The court was assembled at the 50-yard line which allowed for seats to be placed all along the field. Although the Spartans lost 74-79, this event has changed the landscape of college basketball. In 2008, the NCAA's executive committee approved an expanded capacity of stadium's for all semi-finals beginning in 2009. The expectation is to surpass 70,000 fans for the finals of future tournaments. Before the BasketBowl, many did not think a basketball game would be able to draw numbers so large. It was announced on April 15, 2008 that the meeting between Michigan State and North Carolina for the Big Ten-ACC Challenge would become BasketBowl II. This game will take place on Dec. 3, 2008 at Ford Field.

Conference Tournament Answer Key

1) B – 2 (1999 and 2000)

2) D – Al Ferrari (He made 21 of 26 attempts [.808] against Indiana in 1955.)

3) C – 1998-99 (The Spartans finished the season 33-5 for a .868 winning percentage.)

4) B – No (Goran Suton led the team with 38 steals.)

5) A – Japan (Michigan State beat Meija University 63-15 on Jan. 28, 1933.)

6) C – 12 (MSU has had a winning season from 1996-97 through 2007-08.)

7) A – Yes (The Spartans held Bird to 7 of 21 from the field for a .333 field goal percentage.)

8) D – On the banks of the Red Cedar ("...There's a school that's known to all, On the banks of the Red Cedar..." The Red Cedar River flows westward through campus and empties into the Grand River.)

9) D – 31 (The Spartans have not lost a home opener since losing 73-74 to Western Michigan to start the 1976-77 season.)

10) C – 1990s (Steve Smith [First Team in 1990], Shawn Respert [First Team in 1994], and Mateen Cleaves [First Team in 1999 & Second Team in 1998])

11) B – Mateen Cleaves (He recorded 195 steals from 1996-2000.)

12) C – Jay Vincent (He scored 25 points against Central Michigan in his freshman debut on Nov. 28, 1977.)

13) C – Gus Ganakas (He led the Spartans to a record of 89-84 [.514] from the 1969-70 season through the 1975-76 season.)

14) A – Yes (Magic Johnson was drafted number one overall by the Los Angeles Lakers in the 1979 NBA Draft.)

15) D – North Carolina (The Spartans have faced the Tar Heels four times and have lost every meeting.)

16) C – Idong Ibok (His hometown is Lagos, Nigeria.)

17) A – Yes (MSU finished 22-6 in Heathcote's last season [1994-95].)

18) D – Wisconsin (The Spartans lost 63-64 to the Badgers on Jan. 12, 2002.)

19) C – Points ("Watch the points keep growing….")

20) B – Charles Bemies (He coached MSU to a 5-2 record [.714] in the 1900 and 1901 seasons.)

21) D – Ohio State (The Spartans fell 54-63 to the Buckeyes in the last regular season Big Ten game.)

22) A – Yes (Magic was team captain along with Greg Kelser for the 1978-79 season.)

23) A – 22 (Their first appearance was in 1957.)

24) B – 14 (The Spartans lost 14-42 to the Wolverines on Dec. 7, 1940.)

25) A – 1 (Tom Izzo won the award in 1998 after leading his team to a Big Ten Championship and overall record of 22-8.)

26) A – 2 (MSU won both appearances in the NCAA Tournament Championship game [1979 & 2000].)

27) B – 4 (From the 1997-98 season through the 2000-01 season.)

28) D – Rickey Ayala (He played from 1952-54 and helped recruit fellow high school teammate and future Spartan star, Al Ferrari, to Michigan State.)

29) C – 11 (MSU lost eleven straight in the 1964-65 season and finished 1-13 in conference play.)

30) B – No (The best finish for the Spartans was 15-1 in the 1998-99 season.)

31) B – Goran Suton (He scored a total of 39 points [6 vs. Temple, 14 vs. Pitt, & 23 vs. Memphis].)

32) A – 121 (MSU beat Morehead State 121-53 in 1992.)

33) D – 2000-01 (The top-ranked Spartans lost 58-59 to the unranked Hoosiers on Jan. 7, 2001.)

34) D – Marcus Taylor (He led the Big Ten with a 17.7 per game average in the 2001-02 season.)

35) A – Stephen G. Scofes (This trophy was first awarded in 1963 to William Schwartz. Drew Neitzel was the 2008 recipient.)

36) C – Alton Kircher (He led his alma mater to a record of 4-18 in the 1949-50 season.)

37) C – Ken Johnson (He recorded 72 blocks in the 1984-85 season.)

38) A – Bowling Green (The Spartans lost 79-81 to the Falcons in the fourth home game at the Breslin Center.)

39) D – Indiana (Michigan State is 43-64 all-time against the Hoosiers for a .402 winning percentage.)

40) A – Yes (The Spartans beat Wisconsin 70-61 in the last game at Jenison Fieldhouse.)

41) C – 10 (Six games in 2000 and four in 2001)

42) B – Mike Robinson (He won the award in 1974, which is given to the nation's most outstanding player 6' tall or under.)

43) C – Drew Neitzel (He made 251 of 291 career attempts for a .863 percentage made.)

44) B – False (He does have a banner that hangs at the Breslin Center along with the retired jerseys, but his banner says " Head Coach, 1976-1995".)

45) C – Magic Johnson (He appeared on the Nov. 27, 1978 cover titled "The Super Sophs".)

46) A – Sports figures (Figures representing the twelve varsity sports of the school at the time of dedication [1945])

47) D – 118 (He did this over a span of six games for an amazing per game average of 19.7.)

48) A – 1 ("Magic" Johnson was inducted in 2002.)

49) B – 3 (The Spartans came from behind to beat Bradley [27-28 at half, 66-61 final], BYU [25-35 at half, 68-61 final], & Illinois [20-24 at half, 51-41 final].)

50) C – 18 (The Spartans won every Big Ten game from Jan. 9, 1999 to Jan. 20, 2000.)

Note: All answers valid as of the end of the 2007-08 season, unless otherwise indicated in the question itself.

Championship Game *4-Point Questions*

1) Against how many members of the Big Ten does MSU have an all-time winning record?

    A) 2
    B) 4
    C) 5
    D) 8

2) How many consecutive seasons has every Spartan home game been sold out at the Breslin Center?

    A) 3
    B) 5
    C) 6
    D) 8

3) What is the MSU record for largest margin of victory over a Big Ten opponent?

    A) 46 points
    B) 51 points
    C) 58 points
    D) 63 points

4) What is MSU's all-time worst seed in the NCAA Tournament?

    A) 7th
    B) 9th
    C) 10th
    D) 12th

Championship Game *4-Point Questions*

5) Who was Michigan State's first Big Ten opponent?

    A) Michigan
    B) Wisconsin
    C) Northwestern
    D) Illinois

6) Does MSU have an all-time winning record in the Big Ten Tournament?

    A) Yes
    B) No

7) Excluding Michigan, who is the last team from the state of Michigan to beat the Spartans?

    A) Central Michigan
    B) Detroit
    C) Kalamazoo
    D) Olivet

8) Who holds the Spartan record for the most points scored in a freshman year?

    A) Zach Randolph
    B) Chris Hill
    C) Shawn Respert
    D) Magic Johnson

Championship Game *4-Point Questions*

9) Did Michigan State attempt more free throws than its opponents in the 2007-08 season?

    A) Yes
    B) No

10) What is the MSU record for most rebounds as a team in a season?

    A) 1,301
    B) 1,438
    C) 1,521
    D) 1,672

11) Which player holds the MSU team record for most points scored in an NCAA Tournament game?

    A) Drew Neitzel
    B) Jay Vincent
    C) Steve Smith
    D) Greg Kelser

12) What is MSU's all-time winning percentage at the Breslin Center?

    A) .781
    B) .811
    C) .873
    D) .962

Championship Game *4-Point Questions*

13) In which category did Shawn Respert lead the nation in the 1994-95 season?

A) 3-point field goals made per game
B) Total turnovers
C) Assists per game
D) Free-throw percentage

14) How many times has Michigan State been beaten while ranked #1 in the *AP* Poll?

A) 1
B) 3
C) 5
D) 7

15) How many times has Michigan State won 30 or more games in a season?

A) 1
B) 2
C) 4
D) 6

16) How many games did it take Michigan State's Tom Izzo to reach 300 career victories?

A) 374
B) 380
C) 426
D) 451

17) In the 2007-08 season, did any player for Michigan State have 10 or more turnovers in a single game?

A) Yes
B) No

18) How many total weeks has Michigan State held #1 in the *AP* Poll?

A) 4
B) 9
C) 15
D) 22

19) When was the last time the Spartans failed to score 2,000 points as a team in a single season?

A) 1975-76
B) 1980-81
C) 1988-89
D) 1995-96

20) What is the Michigan State record for most consecutive NCAA Tournament losses?

A) 2
B) 3
C) 5
D) 6

21) How many MSU head coaches also played for the Spartans?

    A) 0
    B) 1
    C) 3
    D) 5

22) Which MSU game holds the record for the highest rated televised game?

    A) Indiana State 1979
    B) Duke 1999
    C) Florida 2000
    D) North Carolina 2005

23) Tom Izzo's first collegiate head coaching position was for MSU.

    A) True
    B) False

24) How many Big Ten schools have an all-time winning record against the Spartans?

    A) 2
    B) 3
    C) 5
    D) 6

Championship Game *4-Point Questions*

25) When was the last season MSU's opponents combined to score more points than the Spartans?

    A) 1995-96
    B) 1998-99
    C) 2002-03
    D) 2005-06

26) Has Michigan State broken the 1,500-win mark?

    A) Yes
    B) No

27) How many times has Michigan State been a #1 seed in the NCAA Tournament?

    A) 2
    B) 4
    C) 5
    D) 7

28) Which Michigan State head coach never lost a game?

    A) Charles Bemies
    B) John Kobs
    C) Chester Brewer
    D) George Denman

29) Which decade did MSU have its worst winning percentage?

    A) 1940s
    B) 1960s
    C) 1980s
    D) 2000s

30) Have the Spartans ever scored more than 3,000 points in a single season?

    A) Yes
    B) No

31) How many Spartans have scored 1,000+ career points?

    A) 21
    B) 26
    C) 31
    D) 37

32) Against which major conference does Michigan State have the best record?

    A) SEC
    B) ACC
    C) Pac 10
    D) Big 12

33) What is the MSU record for largest margin of victory in an NCAA Tournament game?

A) 25 points
B) 29 points
C) 34 points
D) 37 points

34) Which Spartan had the best three-point percentage in the 2007-08 season (min. 25 attempts)?

A) Raymar Morgan
B) Drew Neitzel
C) Kalin Lucas
D) Chris Allen

35) When was the last season the Spartans made more than 50% of their shots from the field?

A) 1993-94
B) 1997-98
C) 1999-00
D) 2005-06

36) Has Michigan State ever had four players drafted in the NBA Draft in the same year?

A) Yes
B) No

Championship Game   *4-Point Questions*

37) Who is the only player to lead Michigan State in total points scored for four different seasons?

    A) Mateen Cleaves
    B) Greg Kelser
    C) Shawn Respert
    D) Pete Gent

38) Each of Michigan State's National Championship teams also won the Big Ten regular season.

    A) True
    B) False

39) What is the MSU record for most consecutive seasons with 20 or more wins?

    A) 3
    B) 4
    C) 6
    D) 8

40) Which of the following players did not score over 2,000 career points while at Michigan State?

    A) Steve Smith
    B) Greg Kelser
    C) Shawn Respert
    D) Paul Davis

Championship Game *4-Point Questions*

41) How many Spartans averaged more than 20 minutes of playing time per game in the 2007-08 season?

    A) 3
    B) 5
    C) 6
    D) 8

42) Who was the last Spartan to be named First Team Academic All-American?

    A) Drew Neitzel
    B) Idong Ibok
    C) Drew Naymick
    D) Chris Hill

43) Which decade did the Spartans have the best winning percentage?

    A) 1900s
    B) 1930s
    C) 1990s
    D) 2000s

44) What is MSU's longest losing streak in Breslin Center?

    A) 3 games
    B) 4 games
    C) 6 games
    D) 8 games

45) Who was the last Michigan State player to be awarded Big Ten Defensive Player of the Year?

A) Eric Snow
B) Ken Redfield
C) Shannon Brown
D) Jason Richardson

46) Where did MSU's head coach Tom Izzo play college basketball?

A) Central Michigan
B) Iowa
C) Fresno State
D) Northern Michigan

47) The 1979 MSU Championship team had a higher per game scoring average than the 2000 Championship team.

A) True
B) False

48) How many players have had their jersey number retired by Michigan State?

A) 4
B) 6
C) 8
D) 10

49) Which team did MSU lose to in the 1989 Postseason NIT Tournament Semifinals?

    A) UAB
    B) Fresno State
    C) Syracuse
    D) Saint Louis

50) Which team broke Michigan State's 53-game home court winning streak?

    A) Wisconsin
    B) Minnesota
    C) Louisville
    D) Georgetown

Championship Game Spartan Cool Fact

Michigan State's first Big Ten Champion team and National Championship team played each other on the court at Jennison Fieldhouse. 10,000 raucous fans would fill the arena to cheer on the Spartans. On Aug. 12, 1989, Spartan fans were treated to one final hooray before the doors were closed and basketball was moved to the new Breslin Center. The 1978-79 National Championship team played a team of other former Spartan standouts. The hot August night did not keep the sellout crowd away. What they witnessed was an entertaining game, with Magic Johnson leading the National Championship squad to a 95-93 victory. Johnson had 25 points and 17 rebounds. The undefeated home record of the 1978-79 team would remain intact.

Championship Game Answer Key

1) C – 5 (Ohio State [61-50, .550], Penn State [25-4, .862], Iowa [58-52, .527], Northwestern [76-36, .679], & Wisconsin [66-58, .532])

2) D – 8 (Every home game has been sold out since the 2000-01 season. Out of the 292 total games played at the Breslin Center, 162 have been sold out.)

3) B – 51 points (MSU beat Michigan 114-63 on March 4, 2000.)

4) C – 10th (The Spartans were a 10 seed in the 1985 and 2002 NCAA Tournament.)

5) C – Northwestern (The Spartans beat the Wildcats 67-62 on Jan. 6, 1951 to win their inaugural Big Ten game.)

6) A – Yes (The Spartans are 11-8 all-time for a .579 winning percentage.)

7) B – Detroit (The Spartans fell 65-68 at home to Detroit on Dec. 13, 1997.)

8) D – Magic Johnson (He scored 511 points as a freshman.)

9) A – Yes (The Spartans attempted 661 free throws while their opponents attempted a combined 655.)

10) C – 1,521 (This record was set in the 1999-00 season.)

11) D – Greg Kelser (He scored 34 points against Notre Dame in the 1979 NCAA Tournament.)

12) C – .873 (The Spartans are 255-38 all-time at the Breslin Center.)

13) A – 3-point field goals made per game (He made 119 3-pointers in 28 games for an average of 4.25.)

14) B – 3 (MSU lost 55-57 to #4 Illinois in 1979, 50-52 to unranked Purdue in 1979, and 58-59 to unranked Indiana in 2001.)

15) B – 2 (MSU had an overall record of 33-5 for the 1998-99 season and 32-7 for the 1999-00 season.)

16) C – 426 (Izzo's 300th win came against Iowa on Feb. 23, 2008.)

17) B – No (Freshman guard Kalin Lucas committed a team high seven turnovers against Purdue on Jan. 8, 2008.)

18) A – 4 (Jan. 3, 1979; Jan. 9, 1979; Dec. 26, 2000; & Jan. 2, 2001)

19) D – 1995-96 (The Spartans scored 1,986 points and finished the season 16-16.)

20) A – 2 (The Spartans have lost two straight NCAA Tournament games five different times.)

21) C – 3 (George Gauthier, Lyman Frimodig, & Alton Kircher)

22) A – Indiana State 1979 (The nation tuned in to see what would be the first of many Magic vs. Bird match-ups.)

23) A – True (Izzo's only other head coaching position was at Ishpeming High School [MI] from 1977-78.)

24) C – 5 (The Spartans are 71-91 against Michigan [.438], 51-53 against Illinois [.490], 54-56 against Minnesota [.491], 43-64 against Indiana [.402], and 43-61 against Purdue [.413].)

25) A – 1995-96 (Opponents combined for 2,053 points compared to MSU's 1,986 points.)

26) B – No (MSU has an all-time record of 1,429-991 for a .590 winning percentage.)

27) B – 4 (1990, 1999, 2000, & 2001; Seeding did not start until 1979.)

28) D – George Denman (He coached the Spartans to a record of 11-0 for the 1902 and 1903 seasons.)

29) B – 1960s (The Spartans went 102-124 for a .451 winning percentage.)

30) B – No (The most points MSU has scored as a team in a single season was 2,889 in the 1999-00 season.)

31) D – 37 (Drew Neitzel was the last player to surpass 1,000 career points.)

32) A – SEC (MSU is 29-20 all-time against the conference for a .592 winning percentage.)

33) C – 34 points (The Spartans defeated Pennsylvania 101-67 in the 1979 National Semifinals.)

34) B – Drew Neitzel (He made 97 of 244 from 3-point range for a .398 percentage made.)

35) A – 1993-94 (The Spartans shot 944-1,875 from the field as a team for a .504 percentage made.)

36) B – No (The most players drafted in a single year is three. This happened in 2001 [Jason Richardson, Zach Randolph, & Andre Hutson] and again in 2006 [Shannon Brown, Maurice Ager, & Paul Davis].)

37) C – Shawn Respert (1991-92 [474 points], 1992-93 [563 points], 1993-94 [778 points], & 1994-95 [716 points])

38) A – True (The 1999-00 Championship team also won the Big Ten Tournament [started following the 1997-98 season].)

39) B – 4 (The Spartans won 20+ games from the 1997-98 season to the 2000-01 season and again from the 2004-05 season through the 2007-08 season.)

40) D – Paul Davis (He scored 1,718 career points. Shawn Respert scored 2,531 points, Steve Smith scored 2,263 points, Scott Skiles scored 2,145 points, and Greg Kelser scored 2,014 points.)

41) C – 6 (Drew Neitzel [31.6], Raymar Morgan [27.7], Goran Suton [26.6], Kalin Lucas [25.1], Travis Walton [23.5], & Drew Naymick [21.2])

42) D – Chris Hill (He was named First Team Academic All-American in 2005 and 2004. The only other Spartan to be First Team was Greg Kelser in 1979.)

43) A – 1900s (The Spartans finished the decade 76-22 for a .776 winning percentage.)

44) B – 4 games (The Spartans lost four straight at home in the 1992-93 season.)

45) A – Eric Snow (He won this award in 1995. Ken Redfield is the only other Spartan to have been Big Ten Defensive Player of the Year [1990].)

46) D – Northern Michigan (Izzo played guard for the Wildcats from 1973-77 and was named team MVP for the 1976-77 season.)

47) A – True (The 1979 team averaged 75.7 points per game while the 2000 team averaged 74.1 points.)

48) C – 8 (Scott Skiles [4], Mateen Cleaves [12], Steve Smith [21], Johnny Green [24], Shawn Respert [24], Jay Vincent [31], Greg Kelser [32], & Magic Johnson [33].)

49) D – Saint Louis (The Spartans fell 64-74 to the Billikens.)

50) A – Wisconsin (The Spartans fell 63-64 at home to the Badgers on Jan. 12, 2002.)

Note: All answers valid as of the end of the 2007-08 season, unless otherwise indicated in the question itself.

Overtime Bonus *4-Point Questions*

1) Where did Jud Heathcote coach before Michigan State?

    A) Washington State
    B) Arkansas
    C) Montana
    D) Butler

2) How many times has Michigan State begun the season ranked #1 in the first *AP* Poll?

    A) 0
    B) 1
    C) 3
    D) 4

3) Who was the Spartans opponent in the 2007-08 season Big Ten/ACC Challenge?

    A) Duke
    B) North Carolina State
    C) Maryland
    D) Virginia Tech

4) Did Izzo win his first Big Ten Conference game as head coach of Michigan State?

    A) Yes
    B) No

Overtime Bonus *4-Point Questions*

5) What was the first season a player at Michigan State averaged 20 or more points per game?

    A) 1952-53
    B) 1965-66
    C) 1978-79
    D) 1984-85

6) What is inscribed on the statue of Magic Johnson that sits in front of the Breslin Center?

    A) Possibilities are Endless
    B) Pride, Honor, Courage
    C) Basketball Magician
    D) Always a Champion

7) Which player holds the Michigan State record for most points scored in an NCAA Championship game?

    A) Morris Peterson
    B) Magic Johnson
    C) A.J. Granger
    D) Greg Kelser

8) How many Michigan State players have been drafted in the first round of the NBA Draft?

    A) 10
    B) 13
    C) 16
    D) 21

Overtime Bonus *4-Point Questions*

9) What was Michigan State's original nickname?

    A) Farmers
    B) Trailblazers
    C) Pioneers
    D) Aggies

10) Did Michigan State trail at halftime in an NCAA Championship game they went on to win?

    A) Yes
    B) No

Overtime Bonus Answer Key

1) C – Montana (He was head coach of the Grizzlies from 1971-76.)

2) A – 0 (The highest initial ranking for MSU in the *AP* Poll is #3 [1999-00, 2000-01, & 2003-04].)

3) B – North Carolina State (MSU beat the Wolfpack 81-58. The Spartans are 5-3 all-time in the challenge.)

4) A – Yes (He led MSU to a 75-72 win against Arkansas.)

5) A – 1952-53 (Al Ferrari averaged 20.1 points per game.)

6) D – Always a Champion (The statue was dedicated outside the arena in November of 2002.)

7) B – Magic Johnson (He scored a total of 24 points in the 1979 NCAA Championship Game.)

8) C – 16 (The last players taken in the first round were Shannon Brown and Maurice Ager, both in 2006.)

9) D – Aggies (Although Aggies was the official nickname until 1926, the nickname Farmers or Fighting Farmers was widely associated with MSU.)

10) B – No (MSU led Indiana State 37-28 at half and led Florida 43-32.)

Note: All answers valid as of the end of the 2007-08 season, unless otherwise indicated in the question itself.

Player / Team Score Sheet

SPARTANOLOGY TRIVIA CHALLENGE

Name:_____

Preseason		Regular Season		Conference Tournament		Championship Game		Overtime
1	26	1	26	1	26	1	26	1
2	27	2	27	2	27	2	27	2
3	28	3	28	3	28	3	28	3
4	29	4	29	4	29	4	29	4
5	30	5	30	5	30	5	30	5
6	31	6	31	6	31	6	31	6
7	32	7	32	7	32	7	32	7
8	33	8	33	8	33	8	33	8
9	34	9	34	9	34	9	34	9
10	35	10	35	10	35	10	35	10
11	36	11	36	11	36	11	36	
12	37	12	37	12	37	12	37	
13	38	13	38	13	38	13	38	
14	39	14	39	14	39	14	39	
15	40	15	40	15	40	15	40	
16	41	16	41	16	41	16	41	
17	42	17	42	17	42	17	42	
18	43	18	43	18	43	18	43	
19	44	19	44	19	44	19	44	
20	45	20	45	20	45	20	45	
21	46	21	46	21	46	21	46	
22	47	22	47	22	47	22	47	
23	48	23	48	23	48	23	48	
24	49	24	49	24	49	24	49	
25	50	25	50	25	50	25	50	
___ x 1 = ___		___ x 2 = ___		___ x 3 = ___		___ x 4 = ___		___ x 4 = ___

Multiply total number correct by point value/quarter to calculate totals for each quarter.

Add total of all quarters below.

Total Points:_____

Thank you for playing Spartanology Trivia Challenge.
Additional score sheets are available at:
www.TriviaGameBooks.com

85

Player / Team Score Sheet

Name:_____

Preseason			Regular Season			Conference Tournament			Championship Game			Overtime	
1	26		1	26		1	26		1	26		1	
2	27		2	27		2	27		2	27		2	
3	28		3	28		3	28		3	28		3	
4	29		4	29		4	29		4	29		4	
5	30		5	30		5	30		5	30		5	
6	31		6	31		6	31		6	31		6	
7	32		7	32		7	32		7	32		7	
8	33		8	33		8	33		8	33		8	
9	34		9	34		9	34		9	34		9	
10	35		10	35		10	35		10	35		10	
11	36		11	36		11	36		11	36			
12	37		12	37		12	37		12	37			
13	38		13	38		13	38		13	38			
14	39		14	39		14	39		14	39			
15	40		15	40		15	40		15	40			
16	41		16	41		16	41		16	41			
17	42		17	42		17	42		17	42			
18	43		18	43		18	43		18	43			
19	44		19	44		19	44		19	44			
20	45		20	45		20	45		20	45			
21	46		21	46		21	46		21	46			
22	47		22	47		22	47		22	47			
23	48		23	48		23	48		23	48			
24	49		24	49		24	49		24	49			
25	50		25	50		25	50		25	50			

___ x 1 = ___   ___ x 2 = ___   ___ x 3 = ___   ___ x 4 = ___   ___ x 4 = ___

Multiply total number correct by point value/quarter to calculate totals for each quarter.

Add total of all quarters below.

Total Points:_____

Thank you for playing Spartanology Trivia Challenge.
Additional score sheets are available at:
www.TriviaGameBooks.com

87